ROSES A SHAMROCKS

FROM DORSET TO DONEGAL

EDNA RICE

Illustrations
EDNA RICE

Cover
ROSIE RICE

FIVE CROWS PUBLISHING

First published in the United Kingdom in 2008
By Five Crows Publishing, 18 Shreen Way,
Gillingham, Dorset SP8 4EL
Email: dorsetlive@googlemail.com

Copyright © Edna Rice 2008

Illustrations © Edna Rice

All rights reserved. No part of this publication may be reproduced, stored in a retrieval system, or transmitted in any form or by any means, electronic, mechanical, photocopying, recording or otherwise, without prior permission of the publisher and the copyright holder

British Library Cataloguing in Publication Data.
A catalogue record for this book is available from the British Library

ISBN 978-0-9558604-0-9

Printed in Great Britain by Borcombe SP Ltd. Romsey

Introduction

Edna Rice is undoubtedly a skilled raconteur, a bringer forth of her own experiences, polished once again for herself, and here presented to the reader. Here are episodes from her childhood, through a rural World War II, her marriage and then moving to Ireland. Her family and friends are not simply ghosts moving within a nebulous background but all live again in Edna's recollections.

Edna subtly draws one into the world in which she once lived, breathed, understood and importantly, passionately and profoundly loved. Its essence and fragrance has never departed her. Some of the background to her early life in Dorset was drawn for us in her best-selling book, *1939 A Year in the Rural Dorset Landscape*; in *Roses and Shamrocks* she expands upon previous themes and then takes the reader forward in time. A lovely book for those who love to read of country life at the sharp end, in an England and Ireland of shared common values, and the rhythm of the changing seasons. The work is a perfect vehicle for other writers seeking authenticity, to add colour to their own writing. It is also an ideal source book for those involved in the film and TV industry.

For best results, I suggest, reading the book when you are quite alone and wish to withdraw a little. Make a pot of tea; drink it from a well-polished cup and saucer, possibly with a slice of your favourite cake. Turn down the lights, or preferably light the candles, settle down, sit back and let Edna Rice cleverly draw you into her coterie.

A tale, beautifully told, by a gifted writer.

Jack Skelton-Wallace 2008

Myself, aged three

Melbury Grandparents

Compton Grandmother

The Well

The Shepherd

My mother, Betty and me

ROSES

A Dorset Childhood

1924 –1951

Uncle Joe

Feeding Calves

Melbury Hill & Chalk Pit

The Triumph

Dad by the Yew Tree

Mum and Wuffie

CHAPTER ONE
1924-1930

Buddens Farm

My very first memories are of being pushed in the pram up Buddens Lane on Sunday mornings to my grandparent's home at Houses Farm.

Buddens Lane was a lovely place, and was lined with flowers. In the spring it was yellow with Primroses, and many white violets, with a scent that was out of this world. These were followed by Bluebells and May.

There was a long grass ribbon running up the middle of the lane, and two gates to be opened and shut. In later years I was amazed one day when I opened one of the gates for a passing car, the driver threw me out a few coppers. There were no houses there in those days.

We lived at Buddens Farm. It was on the very edge of Melbury Abbas, with the brook at the bottom of the garden being the boundary with Twyford. There was a lovely pond by the roadside, surrounded by willow trees and full of lots of Tadpoles in the spring.

Sometimes we would travel by pony and governess car, which was the usual means of travel then.

My grandmother brought me to Shaftesbury occasionally, and, if it were raining, we would use a big black umbrella. There was a special little bracket to hold it onto the trap.

On the way back we would sometimes stop at the little shop at Cann and gran would buy me a penny bun. We then passed Cann Mills, where my mother was born, and up Cann Hill, which was very steep, to turn into the avenue which led us to Houses Farm. At the end of the avenue there was a letterbox, and one year there was a nest of Robins inside it.

My grandparents lived with Uncle Joe Miles, a much-loved man and a good farmer. He kept beautiful carthorses, along with carters, cowmen, a shepherd, and all the usual men of a busy farm.

Travelling home from there in the springtime we often called into the field near the top of Buddens Lane, where the lambing pens were set out. Bill Bryant was the shepherd in a movable shepherds hut, with the lambing pens made with hurdles and thatched with straw. I would cuddle the newborn lambs.

My mother always had to be back in good time for milking, my father kept to a timetable and milking was always finished by about six o clock. When I was small I was brought out into the stall when milking was in progress, I suppose my parents could not leave me indoors on my own, so I would have my own little stool and keep well back from the legs of the cows. There were usually calves tied on along the walls waiting to be allowed to suck their mothers, and I pretended to milk them. I always had my small cup and was given a small drop from each cow to drink.

The bull was tied at the end of the stall, and when the cows were gone out he would be lonely, so he struck up a friendship with a little kitten and they always lay down together. Over the place were the bull was tied was a loft. This was a wonderland for me, as it was a sort of dumping ground for things no longer used. In the wintertime everything was usually covered up with hay. One of my favourite things up there was an old pram. It was a sort of cradle on wheels, with carved wooden sides. I also remember a piece of an old bible box with a carved wooden top.

When I was old enough to be left indoors, it was not safe for me to light the lamp; there was no electricity then, so I used to sit in the gathering darkness with my dear doggie friend, a greyhound called Wendy, and look at the pictures to be seen in the fire. We

had a black range, which was polished every Saturday. The front was opened and I could see all kinds of pictures in the red coals. The lamp was always hung in the centre of the room, over the kitchen table so it could not be knocked over.
My toys were nearly all hand-made. My grandfather was a carpenter and he made me a lovely dolls house, a dolls cot, and even a scooter, which I used to play with continuously.
Of course all these things would appear by my bedside on Christmas mornings. I had a big Teddy Bear, which Uncle Harry won at Shroton Fair.
I have not mentioned my other grandparents; they lived at Willis Farm at Compton Abbas. I think I was always a bit afraid of Grandad, but Granny was a great favourite. She was a real Tomboy; I think I turned after her a bit. I heard that when my father was small she used tie him to the plum tree for safety.
Grandad was fond of the drink on market days, but the horse used to bring him safely home from Shaftesbury market.
My grandfather used to live at Buddens in the days when all the land thereabouts belonged to Sir Richard Glynn, and my father was born there in 1898. I have been reading an old agreement, which I found in Dads box, for the letting of Buddens Farm in the year 1892 from Sir Richard Glynn to a Richard Fouracre (what a lovely name!). He must have been there only a short while, as my grandfather was living there before 1898.
Grandad must have had a similar agreement. I can see now why some of the rules used to irk my father when he was young.
I am going to write some of them down:

> 1. The landlord excepts and reserves to himself all trees, saplings, spires, pollards, bushes, gorse wood and under wood (not hedge wood) whatsoever and all minerals, coprolites, stone, flints, clay, marl, chalk, gravel and sand, and all manorial rights and royalties whatsoever with power for himself and all persons authorised by him with or without horses and carriages to enter upon the premises at all times to cut down, dig for, remove and carry away the same and also to enter for the purpose of viewing, and of executing the repairs and ascertaining the state and condition of the premises.

2. *The landlord reserves the exclusive right to all game, hares, conies, woodcocks, snipe, wildfowl, fish and wild animals upon the premises, and the right for himself, his friends, gamekeepers and servants at all times to enter thereon for the purpose of sporting and also of preserving the same.*
3. *The landlord reserves power from time to time on giving not less than 14 days notice in writing to resume any part of the demised premises for any purpose whatsoever, making to the tenant reasonable compensation for actual damage sustained and a proportionate reduction of rent.*
4. *The rent to be £135 per annum.*

5. *The tenant not on any of the lands to sow more than two white straw crops in succession, one of which may be wheat.*

6. *The tenant to cultivate the arable lands in a four-crop system of husbandry, not in any year to crop more than one half of the same to corn or grain, nor more than one sixth to pulse to be harvested (which pulse must be drilled or dibbled and twice hoed) and not more than one acre of Swedes, turnips mangold, mustard, rape or other seed, except three acres of rye grass and clover seeds shall be harvested as a crop, the remainder to be in grass roots or other green crops to be fed off or consumed on the farm.*
7. *The tenant is not to put up any iron or wire in making or repairing any fence.*

These are just a few of the rules on the agreement. The thing my father hated most was the gamekeeper always sneaking up on them. He must have taken a dim view of the rule about conies also.

My father joined the army in about 1915 by putting on his age; I think it was the Second Hampshire Regiment he was in. He had a pet owl, of which he was very fond, and while he was away in the war someone killed it, he was very upset about it.

It must have been soon after this that Grandad went to Willis Farm, Compton Abbas.

In 1919 the lands of Sir Richard Glynn were sold. These were spread over eight parishes and extended to an area of nearly 5550 acres and included 36 fertile dairy and grazing holdings, 6 productive corn and stock farms, 3 water power corn mills, 2 temperance Inns, accommodation holdings, numerous cottages, schools and school houses. The total rental value being about £6400 per annum.

The Dorset County Council bought a lot of the farms, including Buddens. Dad was able to rent it from them, being an ex service man. I always remember the days when Mr. Stamford of the DCC came around, everything had to be tidied up, there was always a tense atmosphere about the place, and this was probably a result of the anxiety state of the Sir Richard Glynn days. Mr. Stamford would come into the kitchen for a drink, and to discuss any improvements needed around the farm. One day they decided to take off the old thatched roof and tile it. It was a dreadful mess; layers of thatch, which had been added to for maybe hundreds of years, were removed. At least we were not so worried then of fire, when I was small we were very careful not to throw any paper on the fire, especially in the dry weather.

All the water had to be drawn up from a well in the garden. It was the most sparkling clear water, the buckets had to be thrown down on ropes, upside down or they would float. The top of the well was flush with the ground, with cut stones forming a circle around the edge. It had a lovely round stone cover with an iron ring, which exactly fitted the top, but it was too heavy to be moved daily so it was usually covered by a sheet of galvanise. In the winter the water for all the livestock of the farm had to be drawn up and be carried the few hundred yards to the stalls. It never froze in the well; the water was about six feet from the top. One of my favourite rooms in the house was the cheese room. It was a very large, large room over the dairy, with a wooden stair going up to it and a trapdoor at the top. The trapdoor always had to be kept shut as it formed part of the floor. It was used as a lumber-room and apple store, also as a spare bedroom. It contained a large tin trunk, full of great treasure as far as I was concerned. I could dress up in the fashion of the twenties and before. There was a big paisley shawl with a fringe, and cast off dresses of all descriptions, as well as my mothers wedding veil and wax orange blossom headdress. I kept most of my toys and books up there. We had to be careful on some parts of the floor, as it used to shake about, but it never gave way in my time.

The dairy was not still used for that purpose, but it did contain a big butter barrel on a stand, which had a handle, on a big wheel to turn the beaters inside. It was not the up and over type, the barrel was lying in a vertical position, it must have held well over ten gallons of liquid. Next to the dairy was the back house, as it was called. It contained a big open fireplace with iron firedogs; there were irons crooks on which a big black iron pot was hanging over the fire. This was usually filled up with spuds for poultry and pigs. There was a flagstone floor and in one corner was a huge copper with fireplace underneath. The copper had to be filled with water from the well on washing days, and there were always faggots of sticks alongside.

It was a great day when my mother bought a gramophone. Of course we had to wind it up and keep a supply of needles. I used to play it continuously when left indoors on my own. I could not read the labels on the records, so mum drew a little picture on each. There was a children's one with a story on each side. On one side was the "Queen Who Came To Tea" and on the other was "Please Mr. Man Don't Shoot Me". I thought they were wonderful. We had no radio or television in those days. The other records included "Misery Farm", "The Man Who Broke The Bank In Monte Carlo" and "Goodnight Vienna".

That gramophone was one of the first modern inventions we had. About this time too, Dad bought a motorbike and side chair. It was a Triumph, and had carbide lamps. Mum and I would sit in the side chair and be whisked away around the surrounding countryside.

CHAPTER TWO
1930-1933

Compton. School in the background

School. That made a very big change in my life. The first morning Dad took me in the sidecar, after that I had to walk the two and a half miles. Compton School was decided on. It was about the same distance as Melbury School, but my other grand parents lived just down the lane by the school and I could go there every day for my dinner. It was only a small school of under twenty children. However, there were two teachers. Mrs. Kirkby was the Head Teacher, she had two daughters at the school, and Mrs. Barnes was the young Infant teacher.
The school playground railings ran alongside the main Shaftesbury to Blandford road. There were very few cars passing then, and every time one came along we would all run to the railings to see it. The Hants & Dorset buses had just began to run then. It was a great thing altogether, everybody knew the two conductors, they were like family friends. Of course, an aeroplane was an even greater novelty. One day when Mum and I were walking in the lane we saw the big airship R.IOI sailing along in the sky. It was quite eerie looking, so huge and so silent.
We had quite a long walk to school, through Twyford and up Hawcombe Lane. There were quite a little gang of us from there.

I soon made friends with the neighbouring children. The Hayters were my best friends, they were a big family, and lived in a lovely old thatched cottage. They often used to come and play with me after school.

We used to find lots of birds nests in the big hedges along the roads. I had quite a collection of bird's eggs, I never took more than one of each sort. Dad climbed to the tops of trees to get the bigger birds eggs for me. It was easy to get the little owls eggs, as every year they laid them on the bare ground under the roots of a big oak tree in the field we called Cowground.

It was only in a heat wave I was allowed to go to school without a coat. How I used to hate that coat, it got in the way of all our games.

There was a blacksmiths shop in Twyford and we used to press against the grimy glass of the window to see the horses being shod. One day the house belonging to the smith caught fire. I remember going across the fields with Dad to see it. It was a very muddy time, and I kept getting stuck in the mud. I lost my boots altogether in the end, and Dad had to retrieve them. When we got to the house it was completely gutted. I think the only casualties were some kittens. It was all rebuilt again afterwards.

I used to enjoy the lessons at school. The one that impressed me the most was about some grizzly bears that lived in the Rocky Mountains. I have never forgotten it, and maybe that is why I have longed to go there ever since.

Our nearest neighbours had two children. On the day the youngest one started school Miss Barnes was telling us about the Prodigal Son, and she asked Jim "What did the Prodigal Son do when he was hungry?" Jim replied, "He ate the pigs grub". Everyone went into fits of laughter at that.

One evening on the way home from school, I suppose I was showing off. I told all the children if they came home with me I'd show them something interesting. Now, at that time, as probably now, you were not allowed to kill a pig without being a properly authorised person and having a licence to do it. Well, the day before, a lovely pig had broke its leg out in the yard, and not wanting to waste it, Dad butchered it, and hung it up to the beam of the dairy. It was supposed to be a top secret. I don't think I realised that at the time, and when Dad came in from the stall there were these children from the whole village surveying the pig, so everyone from miles around knew about it. The air was very blue that night.

Another thing which happened to our pigs. We had a cess pit from the stall in our yard, it was covered over with oak planks, and the pigs loved to sleep on this as it was dry and warm. There was a large number of very big pigs, they must have been a great weight, and the whole thing collapsed with them. They were all trying to swim around in the foul smelling tank, and some of them cut their own throats with their sharp front feet. I can't remember how many were saved.

The biggest event which happened on the farm at this time was the haymaking. On the appointed day for it to begin there was an early start. Uncle Joe would send down a couple of big cart horses and a mowing machine, which was driven by Bill England, the carter. He used to start about 6 O Clock. Dad would have already cut round the outside with a scythe. I used to explore the field, the flowers that were cut off, the frogs and the mice that were made homeless, and sometimes a pheasants' or partridges' nest. After two or three days we would turn the hay by hand. I was not allowed to use a real prong so Dad used to cut one out of the hedge for me, from a nice smooth, forked, hazel stick. I thought that was a great comedown when all the rest were using real ones. Mum always wore a big white sunbonnet with beautiful stitches on it, it must have been an heirloom.

When the hay had dried a bit, before nightfall, it was put into small heaps, which we called pooks. I never heard that word in other parts. When it was shook out again, and really dry, Betty the pony would pull it to the rick on a hay sweep. She always wore a small branch of elder stuck in her bridle to keep the flies off.

About 1930, or maybe a bit before that, there was a slump in farming, I was too young to worry about those things, but Dad took up rabbit catching with a vengeance, as the rent had to be paid for the farm, and there was not much coming in. I remember he bought three cows and a calf from Shaftesbury market for fifty shillings. The man who owned them was desperate, as he had no food for them. I used to drive them down to the pond to drink; one old cow was so quiet she used to let me ride on her back.

From this time on it was rabbiting for me. Dad used to buy up all the rabbits on farms over quite a wide area. They were caught with snares, nets, guns and dogs. There was a very large rabbit population then, and whole fields of corn were ruined by them. Every holiday, and weekend during the winter I was expected to help, and many hours were spent on frosty mornings watching the nets after the ferrets were put in.

The ferrets were special friends of mine; I was always in charge of them. There were white ones with pink eyes and brown polecats. I liked the white ones best, and only remember being bitten once. They will not let go if they do bite, and Dad had to put a lighted cigarette under its' nose before it would let go. Yet, I had no fear of them and used to make pets of them. Sometimes they would kill a rabbit in the hole, and had to be dug out, as the ferret would eat it, and then go on to sleep in the hole.

One day Dad dug a very deep hole, about six feet deep, and we could just see the rabbit's ears. He still could not reach it, so I had to be held by the feet and dropped down the hole headfirst to reach the rabbit. I was very frightened in case I would not get out again.

Another day, after Dad had put down the ferret, out came a big fox with the ferret on its back. It was carried some distance before it fell off. Dad could not shoot the fox without hitting the ferret.

An old man used to come around with a horse and cart to buy the rabbits. He paid from tuppence to fourpence each for good ones. The dairy used to be full of them hanging by the legs from the ceiling.

I became an expert rabbit catcher and even poacher. I became quite proficient at catching rabbits with nothing but my bare hands. I would see the rabbit in its sit, as we used to call it; Now, if you stop, the rabbit immediately runs away; but, if you keep going it will sit tight. So the secret was to just literally fall on it.

Even when I was married I often supplied a nice rabbit for dinner by this method. This was in the days before myxomatosis.

It was great when I learnt to read; I soon read everything in the house. Even when I was quite small I read all of Mums books; Sherlock Holmes, Tom Browns Schooldays, some Ethel Dells, Rider Haggards, and many more.

I was made to read a chapter or two from the Bible before going to bed at nights, and so gradually worked my way through the Bible. I am pleased about it now, as I know more about it than I otherwise would have done.

I was always borrowing books from my friends, and usually read them whilst perched in the boughs of one of the plum trees. I spent most of my spare time in trees, I could see, without being seen, and when the purple plums were ripe it was an added bonus.

One of the plum trees grew near the house, so from there I used to run around on the roofs. Underneath this tree there were lovely Madonna lilies, they must have been there for years, there were so many of them.

About this time my mother became very fond of gardening. Out came all the stinging nettles, old iron, and stones.

All these big operations took place on market days, when Dad was safely out of the way. I would come home from school to see completely different scenes; trees and bushes chopped down and others put in their place. I was raked in to help and became very fond of it too. The garden became very beautiful in a few years, and it ran right around the house.

The house soon became covered with roses and creepers. We had an outside toilet then(which was always crudely referred to as the dyke), and that was covered with Virginia creeper. Sometimes it was a job to shut the door, as the creeper grew all over it. We took no notice of going out there in all weathers and in the dark nights.

We made a rose garden. The hybrid teas came on the scene around that time. So we purchased some of them; Etoile de Holland; Shot Silk; Madame Butterfly, and many more. The patio around the house and out to the gate were made of bricks, all beautifully fitted together with a raised edge, some of which only came to light after we had cleared away barrow loads of weeds. They really set off the garden, but it meant many hours spent weeding them with a kitchen knife.

There was a huge Irish Yew tree outside the back door. It was sometimes covered with red berries, but it was deadly poison, and we had to be careful not to let any animals near it. I kept white Angora rabbits on the lawn, and one day there was a small twig of yew in their run, that was the end of the poor rabbits.

CHAPTER THREE
1933-1939

In 1933 I had to leave Compton School. The numbers had dwindled down to less than fourteen, and so the school was closed. Most of the children went to Fontmell Magna, but it was nearer for me to go to Melbury Abbas.
Unfortunately, both my dear grandparents had died at Melbury before that.
I did not know many of the children there. We used to sit on long forms, and if you were unlucky enough to be sitting at the end the boys would take great delight in shoving you off. Not long after that, however, we got beautiful new desks. Each one was for two people. The desktops used to lift up to give us individual space for our books etc.
There were two teachers there; Mrs. Pritchard, who was very nice, was the Head Teacher, and the other teacher looked after the infants.

TUFTY
Unfortunately, Mrs. Pritchard retired not so long after I went there, to be replaced by Tufty. This was not her real name, of course, but the children never referred to her by any other

14

name. I don't know how the name came about. I'm afraid she was not a very good teacher, and, as she had from eight to fourteen year olds in her class we got very little learning. I always felt cheated over my school days. The new senior school opened in Shaftesbury the term after I left, January 1939.

There was no going home for dinner for the ones a long distance away, so we had to bring our own. I used to cut my own sandwiches (after milking a cow) as Dad and Mum were out milking at that time. We used to take cocoa and sugar in a tin. There was a big tortoise stove, which heated the school, with a large kettle on top of it, so we made our own cocoa. We often toasted our sandwiches on a wire toasting fork. They were always falling in the fire, but we fished them out and enjoyed them just the same. There was no supervision, as Tufty retired to her own house, and the infant teacher went to her sisters' house for dinner.

SCHOOL PRANKS

We were all pretty bored at school. We read every book in the school cupboard, time, and time again. These comprised of "The Pickwick Papers", "The Water Babies", "Coral Island", and a few more.

Tufty never seemed to get around to teaching many lessons. I'm afraid we were always playing tricks, which was mainly a result of sheer boredom. We composed a poem about Tufty, which we sang to the tune of "I Vow To Thee My Country". We sang this song pretty often, and more and more children started to sing the wrong words, so at last Tufty realised what was going on. I think it was after that she decided to get a cane. She used it very frequently, and we had to hold out our hands for so many strokes on each.

Another of her favourite punishments was to stand us in the corner with our backs to the class. We used to spend a lot of time writing notes to one another in class, and if we were spotted we had to show the notes to Tufty. There were lots of knotholes in the floor so we would quickly push them down in these, and the notes would not be found. In after years my husband was doing some building work at the school and he found some of the notes I had written so many years before.

I'm afraid things became really hilarious sometimes. Some of the boys had been to a joke shop and got a quantity of itching powder. This was liberally shaken around Tufty's desk and seat. You can imagine the results!

Also, there was a pencil, which made glass look broken, and this was put on the mirror just inside the cloakroom door. Another thing was snuff. This was given to some unsuspecting child, who was told to sniff. There would be much sneezing, poor Tufty would go berserk!

There were a lot of big boys there at that time and there were often terrible fights in the playground.

Melbury School was situated in a delightful spot, nestling down under Melbury Hill, with the church just across the road from the playground.

There were four huge trees growing in the playground. They were great fun for our games; we could hide behind them or dance around them.

The school also had a garden, where we all had a small plot, and a prize was given each year for the best one.

Next to the garden wall was an old village pound, and next to that again was the pond. This was always a big attraction, especially in frosty weather. The boys took great risks riding their bikes over it. The most exciting time was as it was beginning to thaw. There would be a big loose piece of ice in the centre, and by riding down the bank at speed the bikes went on to it, and a very shaky ride it would be. The bravest and best of those cyclists later died in a Japanese prison camp. I'm sure he was just as brave till the end. Sadly there is no pond there now. Why must they do away with everything in the name of progress?

It was a long walk to school every day, when I went to Melbury School first there were no houses at all for the first mile or so. I used to be really frightened going up the long lane on my own, but I never told anyone that. I was most frightened I would meet a fox, which was strange when I later became so attached to one. The worst thing was I had to view all the wires put down by

Dad to catch the foxes and badgers, which were getting his rabbits. These were put down in runs that were crossing the road. I was terrified there would be one, and sometimes there was. I had to run home to inform Dad who would bring his gun to put the animal out of its misery. All the animals caught during the day were skinned that night, and the skins were sent off to Horace Friend (Wisbech). They were worth about 4/6 to 7/6, old money then. I then had to hurry and get to school on time.
One morning, what did I meet but a herd of elephants! They were from a travelling circus, and all the big animals had to walk from place to place.
Most of my spare time out of school was spent working on the farm or rabbiting. About a year after I started school at Melbury Dad bought some enormous hayricks from Uncle Joe in a field situated down our lane. Every evening I was captured to help with it. The hay had to be cut into square chunks with the hayknife and tied up with haybonds. These were made with a small tool we called a winker, (that could not have been the right name). I had to turn this while Dad fed the hay into it, and then it was tied around the squares of hay to make trusses. We still had our dear Betty then to haul the hay away. I remember well the day she died, it was the same day that King George V died. Dad was drawing up hay from the field (the ricks were all made in the fields then), when poor Betty dropped dead in the shafts. It was the only time I saw Dad cry; she had been such a faithful friend for years.

MOTOR CAR
Dad did not buy another horse. Instead, he bought two motorcars. They were Overlands. I think they were registered about 1920, American. I never saw any other like them before or since. I can't think where Dad got them. One had the body removed and a kind of lorry bed put upon it. The other had a hood which I never saw put up. They had wooden spokes in the wheels, and they did all the farm work for us. We fitted a sweep on them for sweeping in the hay, and the lorry hauled all the mangolds etc. When they became old the spokes in the wheels

got loose in the dry weather, and with a big load on them they went all funny shapes, but they never completely collapsed.
The first time I drove one of them I was only a child. Dad, who was with me, got out to open the gate, which was on steep ground. I drove gaily through and waited until Dad had the gate fastened. However, the car started running back and I could not stop it. Thankfully Dad managed to jump out of the way, but the gate was completely wrecked. I was not allowed to drive for a while after that.
After getting home from school I had to help with the milking. I never had any homework; it was never given during my time at Melbury. On Saturdays in the winter there were always mangolds to be ground, these had to be meticulously cleaned with an old knife first.
Then there was cake to be cracked. We used to buy the cattle cake in big sheets then. With some cotton and some linseed oil, this all had to go through the cake cracker.
If there was a shortage of hay we had to cut chaff. We mixed straw and, maybe some inferior hay, and put it through the chaff cutter, then mixed it with ground mangolds. It was all done by hand in the days before we had the petrol engine. It was a mammoth job preparing all this food for twenty or more cows and heifers.
We also kept quite a few calves. One calf was in a smallish house, and when we went to let it out it could not get out of the door, so the door had to be made bigger.
About this time the Nobles came to Buddens Lane to start a poultry farm. They bought Uncle Joe's fields both sides of the lane. Whilst waiting for their beautiful house to be built they lived in a huge chicken house. I had to bring them a can of milk every morning on the way to school. They had been living abroad, so it was all very exiting for me. The lane was no longer such a lonely place.

SILVER JUBILEE
In 1935 we celebrated King George V's Silver Jubilee. There was a party for us at the village hall. We all received mugs, and the school children were all dressed up to represent British

Monarchs. Although, there were a few non-monarchs such as Oliver Cromwell, and also a few trumpeters, and yours truly was Britannia. We had pillow fights on a greasy pole, and a good time was had by all.

In the evening Dad and I went to the top of Melbury Hill, where a beacon was lit, and there were cider and other drinks to be had. It was very dark coming home and it was difficult finding our way. As we knew the hill so well, I'm wondering if the drink had anything to do with it! There was a huge chalk pit cut out of the hill, which at the time gleamed brilliant white. We used to have to be careful coming down not to step off into space. It's full up now with trees and is fenced off as private property. I wonder if the old chalk-burning house is still there, many a night we sheltered from the rain in it.

FOOT AND MOUTH

Animals played a big part in my life. I seemed to have a kind of rapport with them. It made life very hard for me, as I was very upset when any of the farm animals had to go to the market. One Monday we sent two calves to Sturminster market. Some of the animals there were found to have foot and mouth disease and all the animals had to be killed. Then followed a terrible time as, one after another, the farms all around us contracted the disease and all the animals were destroyed. We lived in constant fear of it. I remember seeing Uncle Joes cows piled in huge heaps in the field waiting to be burnt. We lived like social outcasts for weeks. Visitors were not welcome and we could visit no one else. We were afraid to let anyone step inside the gate in case there were germs on their boots. But, we were lucky.

I don't know how I could have borne it if we had to put any of our cattle down. All our cows were personal friends of mine. I was miserable if an animal was ill.

I kept many pets. At one time it was white mice, just two to start with. They had very big families, and I made quite a lot of money at school, selling them for tuppence or threepence each. Sometimes there were several inside my desk, and some would be inside my sleeves.

I was never caught by Tufty. I loved the wild mice too. There were quite a lot of them at Buddens, and they came out of the wainscoting, and on moonlight nights I would see them running along the bedrail. My mother became fed up with them and made me fill up all their holes with cement. However, I was so afraid they would starve that I took it all out again.

RABBITING

Of course all this time there was still rabbit catching going on, and Dad lost a lot of rabbits to foxes. Many a night I had to accompany him to the fields where the rabbit wires were. We would take up a good vantage point, and Dad would roll up his sleeve, and with his mouth against his arm make a noise exactly like a rabbit squealing.

We would soon see a fox approaching and bang would go the gun. I don't know what the foxhunting fraternity would have said about Dad's nighttime activities! I don't suppose they were ever found out, but the next day another parcel would be sent off to Horace Friend. If there was no school the next day I was sent off to Bedchester shop to post it. I was sent to the shop most Saturdays, which meant a walk each way of two miles, to get Dad's baccy. It was about fourpence an ounce then, and you could buy five Woodbines for twopence.

We never went away for holidays, but we went to the seaside at Bournemouth for a day every summer. Quite a few members of our family went, it was a real Red Letter Day. It meant early milking that day to be in time to catch the 9.30 bus from the top of Buddens Lane. The journey took about two hours. I never remember it being a wet day, and there were always crowds of people on the sands, even in those days.

Shroton Fair was always another must too. We went there in the evening, and we always came home with coconuts.

CHRISTMAS

Christmas was the most memorable day of the year. My mother was organist at Melbury church for many years, so Christmas morning we would be away on our bikes. There was a very nice organ at Melbury, of course it had to be blown by hand, and if no other person was there to do it I would be roped in. On many the choir practice I was there in that dark corner blowing away, and woe betide if the wind was allowed to go down!

We sang lots of carols and maybe an anthem for Christmas. After church we cycled over to Compton Abbas to my Grandparents house. They had moved from Willis to Glyn Farm by that time. However, there was not so much land there, and Grandad was getting old. Two Uncles and an Aunt remained at Willis.

Granny was in her glory cooking a huge goose or turkey, which she had reared herself, and she loved having all her dear boys at home. There was so much food, several kinds of meat, and of course, Christmas pudding.

Granny would be prevailed upon to sing a song, and she usually dressed up for the part. She would sing "Down on Misery Farm", "Little Old Lady", and "The Isle Of Capri", amongst others.

In the afternoon we had to be away to do the milking. If the weather had been favourable before Christmas the cows would still be out in the fields in the daytime, this saved a lot of work not having to let them out to drink, and cleaning out etc. We would have got in enough food to keep them going for a couple of days.

When this was done it was away on the bikes again to Grannies for Tea. This would be a really gargantuan spread, with meat, trifles, Christmas cake and mince pies. How did we eat it after all that dinner?

Wireless sets had just begun to get popular then, though I remember the "cats whiskers" we used to have before that. There would have to be perfect silence for the six o'clock news and weather.

After tea were games. It used to seem strange to me to see grown ups playing games. Dad was the life and soul of the party, which I could not believe at all. For the rest of the year he was much too busy for such trumpery, as he would call it. I expect that Grannies homemade wine had something to do with it!

It would be late when we reached home, but we had to be up early next morning as Boxing Day was always a rabbiting day.

The Uncles came out with us that day, so milking was done early again. Then away we would go with dogs, guns, ferrets, nets etc. We had two greyhounds at that time, and great dogs they were. There were not many rabbits that could escape them. They were kept on the leash until the guns had had their chance. Any rabbit that had escaped was soon caught up with. They would catch anything they were sent after, including hares, foxes, and even other dogs that were trespassing too much.

One day I was quite frightened when they were chasing a hare. A hare cannot see anything straight in front when it is running, it's eyes are at the sides of it's head. The chase was making a direct beeline towards me at great speed, but, thank Goodness, just in time the hare turned. They are great at quick turning; this will sometimes save their lives.

If there were no ferrets lost we would be back home in time for milking, and were off once again to my Aunts house, where she would have a big cooked dinner for the rabbiters, and another party night.

If any ferret was lost Dad spent some time digging or waiting. In the end, if no ferret was found Dad would get some nice dry hay and make a nest inside the rabbit's hole, then all the holes were stopped up, and, with any luck, next morning the ferret would be asleep inside.

If any ferrets did escape they were quite likely to catch someone's hens. A few hens were kept on most farms then, and there were no battery hens. Most cottages kept some too, and most cottages had a pigsty built on to it.

The worst things I remember were the snakes, I was terrified of them. They were mostly grass snakes, and quite harmless. There was a big tree stump up the lane, and when the sun shone it was a favourite place for a snake. It would drape itself all over the stump, and I would run past it as fast as possible.

One day, when I was walking by our manure heap, I trod on a snakes tail, and it immediately rose straight up and looked me in the eye. I avoided that spot for the rest of the summer.

We had a few Adders around too. Nearly every year one of the cows would get bitten, always on the leg. I suppose they stepped on the snakes. The leg would swell up like a thick

gatepost, and the cow would nearly go dry. However, after a week or two it would be all right again.
I used to love going to the fields to bring in the cows in the summertime. Their hoofs made lovely little bare paths through the grass, which were lined with buttercups and daisies and lots of meadow flowers. In the spring, if we could cover seven daisies with one foot we knew that spring had arrived.
The arrival of, first, the chiffchaffs, then the swallows (the earliest date for them was about the third of April), followed by the cuckoo (about the sixteenth of April) were occasions of great excitement. Whoever first saw a swallow or heard a cuckoo would run to tell the rest of the family, and all would try to see and hear it too. So many people nowadays seem quite unaware of these happenings.

GRANNIE
Every autumn my grandmother would come down for the day, and she and I would go blackberrying and nutting, and maybe we would find some mushrooms. She loved to be outdoors, and would climb trees to pick apples, even up to a short time before her death, when she was over seventy.
I never saw her without a black velvet band around her neck, which had a small stone, possibly a diamond, in the front of it. She was very nice looking when she was young, and her light brown hair never turned white.
She did not believe in wasting time. Any spare time was spent making rugs, patchwork quilts, etc.
She had a very large house, and I often saw her sweep up the floor and quickly flip the dust under the end of the carpet.
One day, the Rector came to call, and she was not dressed to receive him. So she thought she would hide behind the sofa and he would go away again, but he came and sat down to wait for her. Poor granny could not come out for ages!
My schooldays came to end when I was fourteen years of age. My mother wanted me to attend the girls' high school in Shaftesbury, but my father did not agree, there was too much to be done on the farm!

CHAPTER FOUR
1939-1945

Wuffie

THE WAR
Just a few months after I left school the War started. Most of the young men from the village joined the army.
Dad rented some land from the poultry farm and we grew potatoes, mangolds, and rye up there. I remember someone from a jam factory bought our mangolds. I suppose they mixed them with the fruit to make it go further.
There was a big military hospital built not far from us at Guys Marsh, and the poultry farm supplied them with chicken. I worked there for a few hours every week, helping with the plucking and dressing of poultry. I was only paid one and a half penny each for plucking and two pennies each for dressing. To make much money at that meant speedy work, and sometimes I would be plucking the second bird whilst the first was still kicking on the bench.

WAR IN THE AIR
While we were engaged at this there were sometimes air fights. During the Battle of Britain we watched the Spitfires and the Messerschmitts battle it out. It became a Sunday afternoon entertainment (if that is the right word) for my friends and I to

cycle around and view the crashed planes. There were no guards on the planes; they were just left where they fell. We would often climb into the cockpits and bring home bits for souvenirs. One Sunday they had just taken the dead crew out of a German bomber when we arrived.

We also used to go and see any bomb craters. We were not in any target area, but they used to drop the bombs to get rid of them, especially if the planes had been hit. There were two unexploded bombs near our footpath to Compton. When these were dug out we were amazed at the size of the holes, as big as a small house. The holes were dug out in perfect squares to one side of the bombs. You could see the shape of the bombs and the side of the holes where they were lifted out.

There were also bombs dropped near the military hospital, and in Melbury in the watercress beds.

At this time there was a call for aluminium to make planes. Everyone handed in their saucepans and anything else in the house they could find made with aluminium.

THE HOME GUARD

About this time too the Home Guard was formed. Nearly all the men, including my father, joined it. I'm afraid they were a little too enthusiastic, and when they had a mock battle with some regular soldiers the soldiers had rather a rough time. The Home Guard did not have much equipment at first, so my Father fished out his First World War helmet, which Granny was growing flowers in at the time, and wore that.

We had a few frightening times. One day when Mum and I were in the barn a German plane straffed the whole place with machine gun bullets.

If the Germans invaded England the church bells were to be rung. One night there was a scare, all the Home Guard were called out. There was just Mum and me at home and we heard the church bells ringing. We thought the Germans were coming, so we crept up to bed and put the double-barrelled gun under the pillow. We heard a couple of bombs in the distance and we thought it really had happened.

The first thing we did when we got downstairs in the morning was to turn on the wireless for the news. They never mentioned it! We never found out what really happened that night. The Home Guard came back the next morning, the most of them being on Melbury Hill all night. They knew nothing either.

WUFFIE

It was about this time I got my fox!

There was a man near us who knew I wanted to get one, an abandoned one.

Then one day he appeared with a little animal. It seemed it was born in a hedge, and a dog had basked it out.

"You will never keep it alive" said he, which made me determined that it would stay alive.

The little cub was only newly born, no bigger than a baby kitten, blind and helpless. We used to feed it with a teaspoon of milk every hour or so. We did not dare to stop, day or night. Mum was very good to get up in the night to help.

It was a little dog fox and its tummy was perpetually wet. In spite of washing it, and putting on talcum powder after every feed, we still could not do the job of the mother fox, licking it to keep it clean.

However, it survived a few weeks and grew bigger. Though the wetness finally made his back legs paralysed, and it was heartbreaking to hear its little cries. He would drag himself along with his front legs.

I was really desperate by this time. Out in the rickyard a straw rick we were using was nearly finished, and there were a lot of mice at the bottom. I managed to catch some of these mice and fed them to Wuffie (as he was called, although I don't know how he got that name). So for a few days he had a mouse a day. It was like a magic cure, he came to life and never looked back. However, he never ate another mouse for the rest of his life.

When Wuffie was three or four months old I used to put him in a long wire run during the day, but he was never happy. I was very worried, as I did not dare let him out in the wild as, being partly tame, he would probably be shot or killed. But I could not bear to see him unhappy.

As it turned out, it was a lucky chance when he managed to escape one day. We knew he was not safe on his own, we would see him running around, but he would not come up to us. I began to get even more worried than before.

Dad decided, after four days, that we must catch him. So he put down a snare, that we were to watch continuously. Sure enough, Wuffie was soon caught. Poor Wuffie was nearly starved, as I don't think he had found any food. He was so pleased to come home with us, and for thirteen years after that he never tried to run away again. He really loved us and we really loved him.

Although - he never lost his nervousness. If he was frightened he would jump up in my arms and put his little front paws around my neck.

He had the run of the house. He always spent his evenings sitting by the fire, in the best armchair if possible (immediately someone got up from a chair he was in it, and the screams he would make if you tried to get him out again). If strangers came he would dive under the sofa. There would be a look of utter amazement on their faces when Wuffie emerged. It was good enough for a pantomime.

He was a great pickpocket; he would have a tobacco pouch or anything similar and be gone under the sofa in a flash.

He loved sweet things. I was afraid he would lose his teeth as everyone gave him sweets from their precious rations. Every birthday (13 March) we made him a cake, even at the height of the rationing. He was the most important, and the cleverest member of the family. He knew every word we said, especially if someone mentioned bedtime, and then he was gone to hide!

We put him in an old pigsty at night, and when we were working during the day he could go in and out as he pleased there.

The one thing we were frightened of was the hunt. If there were any sound of the hounds we would go running from wherever we were to shut in the fox.

One day the horses and hounds came up the lane and reached the house before we heard them. They came through our yard at just the same time as I reached Wuffies house. The hounds passed within two or three yards of Wuffie and never knew he

was there, they just ran straight past. Why did they not get his scent I wonder?
Wuffie didn't smell, however, and we would never know that he was in the house. One day he sat on the windowsill when the hunt went down the lane. I don't know if they saw him eyeing them or not.
I think I must be getting ahead of time, as there was no hunting during the war.
Wuffie used to have great fun with the dog and cat; they used to chase one another around the table. They would go faster and faster, it was a mad merry-go-round!
We had a evacuee boy of about twelve years old staying for a while during the war. He had come from Walthamstow. He always wore white gloves, and would walk around the farm holding his nose. He did not like the smell of manure, but he became very fond of Wuffie. The two of them would wrestle on the floor. Such screams were never heard before from a fox, they had such fun! I wonder does he remember now the days he spent at Buddens Farm with a fox.
It must have been about the beginning of the war, or just before, that Dad bought a tractor. It was the second one to be seen around our neck of the woods, Uncle Joe had the first one. It was a Fordson, and it made a great difference to us, we could do the heavy work whatever the weather.
There was no cab on it like nowadays, and it was very cold sitting on it all day chain harrowing or some such job.

PIGS
My Father kept a lot of pigs during the war; he would go off to market and buy maybe twenty pigs. There was some law at that time; they had to be isolated from other pigs for so long. We had several other such lots of pigs. They used to go out in relays, as they could pick up a lot of food foraging around the fields.
The food for livestock was rationed then. There were lots of acorns around the fields for them to eat, but the place they most wanted to go was the orchard, especially just before cider making time. If one got in they all would follow, but would they

go out again? It was just like a circus getting them out. I was thoroughly fed up with pigs at that time.

Another time some pigs got across the brook and, for some reason, they would not come back across the water. We had to walk several miles with them to get to a bridge where they would cross.

Ringing the pigs was a terrible job, especially a large sow. We would have to get a rope around her nose and tie her up to a beam. The noise was deafening! We had a special tool to hold the rings, which had to be forced into her poor nose. If we did not do it they would have the whole farm routed up.

During the war we used to share the haymaking with our neighbour up the road, Mr. Kift. We would have our tractor and he would have his mule. It usually fell to me to drive the mule for raking or swathe turning. It was a very strange animal, sometimes it would go and sometimes it would not. I found out about the expression "as stubborn as a mule"!

Mr. Kift was a very taciturn type of man; you would get very few smiles out of him. He also had a little evacuee boy named Dennis, who was a great help to him on the farm.

Dennis was always singing the song "Deep in The Heart of Texas". Mr. Kift usually built the ricks, often with Dennis and myself helping. When we got near the top of the roof of the rick it was quite frightening as the space got smaller and smaller, and we seemed so far off the ground. Dennis didn't seem to mind though. He would sing away "the stars at night are big and bright", when suddenly Mr.Kift would come in on the last line in a deep voice, "Deep in The Heart of Texas". No one had ever heard him sing before, we were so surprised he could do such a thing we nearly fell off the rick!

We were always glad when haymaking was over, though we did not very often make bad hay. Dad was a great farmer. He was a pretty good weather forecaster too, and would always wait for the best time to mow. Of course when we got the tractor we soon got machinery to go with it, and mowed our own fields. Dad usually had a rick left over, in case of the next year being a bad one.

He always aimed to have more than half the hay left on Candlemas Day. "If Candlemas Day be fair and fine half of winter left behind" was a very true saying. There were quite a lot of sayings then, I never hear them nowadays.
About corn: "Wheat should cover a hare in March"; "May doesn't go out without a wheat ear"; "Cuckoo oats are no good". Then there was a very true saying "Fogs in March, Frosts in May", and "When the wind is in the East its neither good for man nor beast".
We always got the East wind in April, which would burn up the early grass. This was referred to as a "blackthorn winter". The weather was always bad when the Blackthorn was out. We longed to turn the cows out of the houses, but sometimes it was well into May before we would dare, as once they tasted the early grass they didn't like going back to hay.
There was no strip feeding then. It was always a great day when the cows went out, an end to all those chores!
The cows were so excited too; they would gallop around the field and kick up their heels in delight.
I used to love all our cows. They all had such different characters. I loved tucking my head into their nice warm bodies at milking time, it was a nice rest too. Of course, there were always a few that would give an odd kick. One day, myself and the bucket of milk landed by the back wall!
Sometimes Dad would buy a new heifer and calf from Shaftesbury market. It was usually my job to milk them for the first time. I never minded it a bit then. I'd never do it now.
We had one old cow called Orange; she had belonged to my Grandfather. We always kept her calves. They would always be heifer calves, and they made lovely cows. She was over twenty years old and Dad would never part with her, she was such a good cow. The last three years of her life she had no calf, but she never went dry. Most of the time she would be bringing up a couple of calves, she took to them all as though they were her own.

OUR WORKING DAY

Our days started about 6 O'clock, to get the milking done in time for the milk lorry, which usually came about eight. The churns had to be measured and labelled, and we had to give a hand to lift them onto the lorry.

When I was young we used seventeen-gallon churns. They must have been very heavy to lift, but in later years it was always ten gallon churns.

After milking we washed all the buckets, and washed down the stall, then fed all the animals there were about the place.

Dad was always moving the hen houses to different places around the farm. I had to go and let the hens out and feed them. A trail of animals followed me; dogs, cats, hens, ducks, geese, calves and pigs. They followed me everywhere!

After this we would go in doors for a good breakfast of rashers and eggs, all home grown.

Pig killing was one thing I never helped with. My Grandmother really enjoyed it though, and she never missed that day. She would make masses of brawn, black puddings and chitterlings (chidlins we called them).

CIDER

My Father made quite a lot of cider every year. As well as our large orchard, he would buy up orchards of apples, and we spent days picking them up. We waited until they were ripe enough to fall, or to be shaken off of the trees. A few bruises didn't matter to the cider. We put them into bags and carried them home.

When all were gathered in we put them through an apple mill, after that they were put into horsehair bags. The horsehair would withstand great pressure, and the bags seldom broke. The bags were piled up under the press. About four or five bags went in at a time, and the big screw would force all the juice out as we kept screwing away. There was a hole in the floor containing a large tub, underneath the cider press, to hold the juice as it was squeezed out.

This process was repeated twice. The second press was the clearest and the sweetest. The cider was then strained into large

hogshead barrels, where it would stay to mature. New cider is very sweet to drink. The remains of the apples were called pumice; they were fed to the animals.
When visitors came to the house they were always offered cider, it was very much enjoyed! My Father drank a quart of it every day of his life. In the winter he used to heat it in a saucepan with some sugar and ginger. I think he would have died without it, to keep away the colds.
While the farm work was going on, in a seemingly normal way, the war was still with us. We all became used to it, it was a way of life. We became used to putting up the blackouts each night on all windows. Sometimes I was so tired going to bed I would just undress in the dark. We only had lamps and candles then. I would often burn the candles down low reading in bed. In the stalls we used hurricane lanterns.
Of course, we had rationing too, but we were luckier than some as there were always plenty of milk and potatoes. But nearly all food was rationed, and we learnt to go without sugar in our tea. Cigarettes were also rationed, which was not so good, as was petrol and animal feed. A lot of animals were quite used to being hauled around the locality, as farmers were allowed extra petrol for necessary farm journeys. They'd always have the excuse that they had to take the animals someplace. They were often to be seen outside the pub!
It was not all work though. We had lots of other distractions. There were often socials and dances in the village hall. Most people were in uniform of one form or another. Towards the end of the war there were Americans everywhere, everything was building up to D Day. We were not allowed to go anywhere near the sea without special permits. Every lane that was wide enough was full of tanks and guns, camouflaged by the thick hedges, waiting for the time to strike. Soldiers, even going up to Compton to see my Grandmother, challenged us.
The first night this happened I was lucky not to be shot, I thought that it was just a joke when the soldier said, "halt", however, I realised just in time.
The main roads at this time were a never-ending stream of American tanks and armoured cars. As they passed they used

to throw us out packets of lucky strikes and camel cigarettes. We knew the Germans would not be able to hold out against such force. We made many friends amongst the Yanks. We used to dance to the tunes of "Blaze Away", "12th street rag", "In The Mood" and many more. The Yanks taught us to Jitterbug. We missed them when they left and wondered if they survived the Normandy landings.

MOTOR BIKE
It was around that time I got my first motorbike. It was a BSA, although not a very reliable bike, and I sometimes had to push it up hills. My Father was not pleased with the idea of me having it, so when the man from the cycle shop brought it he had to beat a hasty retreat, and I was left to find out how to ride it by trial and error. I soon learnt, however, and it made a big difference to my life, although petrol rationing curtailed things a bit.
I had a very good friend called Doreen, and we went everywhere together. We joined the Young Farmers Club, and we enjoyed going around the local farms in the summertime. We were also in the church choir. I used to love the Harvest Festival the best. The Harvest hymns are so lovely.
I was all this time very fond of the garden, and as time went on I began to begrudge time spent away from it. The first seeds of my gardening life were beginning to take root.
At last the war came to an end. There was great rejoicing when VE Day came, and then later VJ Day.
We were dancing in the street in Shaftesbury that night. We could throw away the blackout curtains; at last we were all lit up. Though, there were many sad homes where the boys would never come home.

CHAPTER FIVE
1945-1951

Winterfield

Life began to change in many ways after the war. Although things seemed to go on as usual, it was an illusion. There were more forms to fill in, and more machines to do the work on the farm. There was also no more great need to do your bit, to grow your own food, to dig for victory.

It was not too long after the war that I met my future husband. I did not realise that for quite a while of course. Doreen and I were at the village hall, and there was this stranger. As is usual in small places, everyone wanted to know who he was. It was not long before we discovered that he was working on a local farm, and that he was Irish.

I do not know why anyone or anything Irish has such an attraction for me, but it's always been so. I suppose it was all leading up to our life in Donegal in the distant future. We met now and then over the next couple of years.

Around this time, too, I started my gardening career. I began working for Sir Charles Lidbury at Winterfield, which is at East Melbury. It is a lovely place, with rolling downs surrounding it on almost three sides. Sir Charles was a great lover of Daffodils. The garden was a beautiful picture in the springtime, and was visited by the Gardening Association and other organisations.

There were about four acres of pleasure grounds and a farm where Jersey cows were kept for the house. I was pleased to discover that the person in charge of the cows was none other than my old friend Bill Bryant, who used to be Uncle Joes shepherd. He also did the lawn mowing.

I was told, after I left that they named one of the cows after me. I didn't know if it was an honour or not!

Mr. Hinton was the Head Gardener. He was a very knowledgeable gardener, having been apprenticed on a big estate. I was taught gardening as it should be done, and not farmer fashion, as Mr. Hinton used to call it. Farmers very seldom make good gardeners. The first job I did there was preparing seed boxes, and sowing early seeds.

I had got a better motorbike by this time, a Royal Enfield 250. I really loved that bike; it brought me everywhere.

I was able to travel further afield to see all the countryside that had been denied me all through my teens on account of the war. The only time it let me down was the first time Doreen was riding behind. Doreen, for some reason, had that sort of affect on everything. We were going up a steep hill when the bike caught fire. We desperately tried to put out the flames, but to no avail. We were giving up in despair when two men with a car arrived on the scene and put the fire out. Doreen was always accident-prone. If she sat on a gate it would, often as not, collapse. If she rode a bike she usually fell off. We had great laughs about everything though!

Mr. Hinton was a churchwarden at Melbury church, and was also in the choir. We somehow got the idea how marvellous it would be to convert Bill to go to church. We made a real campaign of it and lost no opportunity to cajole and plead with him, but we were never successful.

It was only a few short years afterwards poor Bill was brought there in his coffin.

The three and a half years I spent there was among the happiest of my life. Sir Charles and his two daughters were kindness itself.

We started at seven thirty in the morning, and at ten o'clock we repaired to the bothey (Mr. Hinton's word), for our lunch. Sir

Charles sometimes joined us there; on the days he did not go to London, where he was involved in banking. We would have great discussions on anything and everything. I remember one day telling Sir Charles, after some discussions about money, that it was easier for a camel to go through the eye of a needle than it was for a rich man to enter the kingdom of Heaven. I must have had a great cheek for that, but he took it in good part. One of his favourite ideas was that people were like cheese mites, and the World was the cheese, and as the cheese mites had no inkling of what went on outside their little world, so we had no idea what went on outside our own world. But we were very busy in our gardening world, which was very hard work yet very rewarding.

Sir Charles wrote the following words by Swift in my autograph book, I think they about summed up my own attitude to life: "Whoever could make two ears of corn, or two blades of grass, to grow upon a spot of ground where only one grew before, would deserve better of mankind and do more essential service to his country than the whole race of politicians put together".

MARRIAGE

After three and a half years I left Winterfield to get married. I got plenty of advice on getting married from the men working there! I had always worked with men, so didn't mind their down to earth way of talking.

I missed them all very much. I always remember Sir Charles' laughing face when Mike and I came down the aisle at our wedding on the wrong side of each other.

There was one member of our family that was not so pleased about Mike and I, and that was Wuffie. He tolerated Mike pretty well, until one day he put his arm around me, and in a flash Wuffie bit Mikes' arm, not badly, but just enough to say keep off. This was the only occasion that Wuffie bit anyone. Although, there were about three people, including one of my uncles, that Wuffie did not like at all. When any of them came to the house I shut Wuffie in, to be on the safe side.

However, Wuffie attended our wedding reception wearing a big white bow, and sampled some of the wedding cake. I left him in my mothers care, as poor Wuffie was twelve years old then, which is quite old for a fox. It was much better for him to stay in familiar surroundings for the rest of his life. He died of old age at thirteen years.

The Time of My Life

As I stand and look before me
Through grey and soft blue haze
I see the patchwork of my life
The years, the months, the days

Melbury Hill, the centrepiece,
Stitched all around by trees;
The little patches of green fields,
Like waves upon the seas.

There's Shaftesbury on its' hilltop,
And Melbury, in-between,
With Duncliff on the other side –
A patch for every scene

The first bright patch for Houses Farm,
The place where I was born
The granaries on saddle stones
Were filled with golden corn

Some patches spotted red with cows
And some with black and white
The Harvest time brought fields of gold
Golden, green and white.

In winter time the scene is changed
The colours fade to grey
My lovely hill is white with snow
It's time to go away

The time of life is overAnd youth had fled away
But memories of the patchwork quilt
Are all I have today.

Home Guard

Cows in the Yard

The Overland

The Milk Lorry

Myself, with Dog, Fox and Cat

Sir Charles

Bill and Mr. Hinton

Mr. Hinton in the Melon House

Doreen & I on the Enfield

Mike and I at Buddens

SHAMROCKS
PART ONE
The Wexford Boy

Ireland 1912-1947

*The Rice family circa 1912
(mikie is the little child upon his Mothers' knee)*

CHAPTER SIX
1912-1915

Fair day at the cross in the Irishtown

In the year 1912 a little boy was born in a place called the Irishtown. His name was Michael Rice, Mikie to all his friends.
The Irishtown is at the top of a steep hill, on which New Ross in the County Wexford was founded.
It has a very wide street, where, up until about thirty years ago, the monthly fair was held. It is said that years before there was another row of houses in the middle of the present road.
There are trees planted along the sides of the street, Michaels' uncle put them there many years ago. They are, sadly, lopped by the council every year, so they have rather a dumpy appearance. The road runs up to the top of the hill, culminating at the graveyard and the Good Shepherd convent (now the Mercy convent).
The house where Michael was born is the oldest in the Irishtown. It is slated and has an arch shaped top over the front door. The little windows are much as they were in the old days. There is a larger doorway leading through to the back, where years ago a bacon curing business was carried on by John Rice, Mikies great great grandfather. This was connected to the export business on New Ross quay in the Seventeenth century.
John Rices' cousin Edmund, the beloved founder of the Christian Brothers, probably had an interest in this, as at that

time he had a large export business in Waterford, and used to visit New Ross quite a lot. Bacon was one of the main products exported, mostly to Newfoundland.

John Rice came to a very sad end at the Battle of Ross in 1798. It is said he hid many people in the lofts of his bacon curing sheds during the fierce fighting in the town. When the enemy retook the town the soldiers came to his door to find the fugitives. He stood in that arched doorway and blocked their path, whereupon one of the soldiers drew his sword and tried to kill him, but he managed to hold the sword in his teeth and throttled the soldier. He was then overpowered and taken to the cross, just down the road, and shot.

We do not know the details of what happened to the poor people who were hiding in the lofts. There were so many people killed in New Ross that day, they probably met the same fate. However, Johns' wife and three children (two girls and a boy) managed to escape. This little boy, another John, became Mikies great grandfather.

When this John was twenty years old he married a girl from near New Ross, her name was Margaret Murphy.

They then sailed across the sea to Liverpool, where they boarded a sailing ship, the "Miles Barton", bound for Melbourne, along with 340 other passengers. This was just a year before the first steamship, the "Great Britain", sailed to Melbourne.

After landing at Melbourne they made their way to a place called Silver Springs Creek, near Beechworth, which was a gold field. They must have had a very hard journey there; we do not know if they had any transport there or if they walked the rough country.

They spent six years working at the goldfield, and must have had moderate success. Unfortunately, poor John caught a sickness, through working in the cold snow waters from the high mountain ranges nearby, and died, leaving his wife with three little boys. Taking the small fortune her husband had made she came back to New Ross on a sailing ship.

She went to live with her sister, Sally, who had a shop and a public house in the Irishtown, just below her father-in-laws' house. This house stood in the middle of where the Wexford-

Kilkenny road now runs. Her son eventually returned to live in his fathers' old home, a few yards up the street.

This John was Mikies father. He was fifty years old when he married a girl from the public house near the long meadow in the Irishtown. Her name was Mary Gantley.

She had had a very hard life, as both her parents had died when she was a young girl. Being the oldest of a family of ten children, she promised her mother on her deathbed, she would look after them all.

She was a pretty girl with dark auburn hair, and her family all loved her. She lived with them until they all grew up. She was about thirty years old when she married to have a big family of her own.

The Rice's were quite well off in those days with quite a lot of houses and land. Mikies father, however, did not take after the earlier members of the Rice family, who were great businessmen, as he liked a good time with his friends in the pubs. Yet he had a very kind nature, and would give away the shirt off his back.

It was not a good time for Mikies mother, who watched their fortune dwindle away.

Michael was the seventh surviving child, and there was one more sister after that. When Mikie was three years old he was sent to school run by the Carmelite Sisters.

He still remembers his first day at school, where one of the nuns (I suppose to keep him quite) took him outside to pick daises. She picked off the petals of the daisy one by one saying "now you love me, now you don't". He was very young to start school.

One day his eldest sister was going to give him a bath. He protested loudly, and when she had got him undressed he managed to escape and ran naked out of the door and across the street to an old woman called Nora Corbett, who took pity on him and gave him a penny.

The children of the house must have been very excited to look out into the street on fair days. From an early hour the street would be full of animals, mostly cattle and horses. There were carts of all descriptions. Most of these were flat bodied, with creels, which could be fitted on to make a kind of slated cage, with a sliding door at the back for carrying the smaller animals. Most of the men wore dark clothes, with hard hats, while most of the women wore shawls.

There would be much bargaining, and luck money would be given. There were usually a few IRA men there, also agents of the landlords, who usually had superior horses to ride. There were many things on sale; farm produce, gates, ladders etc. Of course, there was no tarred road in those days; the road was hard trodden stone.

The sounds of the fair must have been very exciting for the children. Clip-clop of horses hoofs, blaring cows, raised voices, the barking dogs, and maybe the sound of a fiddle would be heard from the open doors of the many public houses. The people of the Irishtown must have got plenty of free manure for their gardens when the fair was over! There were sometimes hundreds of cattle at the fair, and they were mainly at the lower end of the Irishtown. Up above, in the Bosheen area, were many Tinkers with donkeys for sale.

It was a noted horse fair also, from the Bosheen up to the graveyard. Here there was a field called the long meadow, where buyers would bring horses for ringing. They were driven around in a ring for testing their wind and movement.

Mikies aunt still lived in the public house nearby, which had been his mothers old home. They must have done good business in those days, many deals would have been made in the little back room. There were buyers at the fair from Dublin, Northern Ireland, and even from England. It was one of the biggest horse fairs in the South East.

Mikie left the Irishtown when he was three and a half years old, to live at Ballymacar, about two miles outside the town.

CHAPTER SEVEN
1915-1926

Ballymacar

Mikie was delighted to go to Ballymacar, there was never failing interest here for children. It was a lovely farm of about sixty acres, with very good land. The house was situated about a quarter of a mile from the road. There were double gates going in, with big round stone piers at each side, on top of which were white marble stones. A stile was built into the stone wall at the side, which the children always jumped over. Further down the avenue, as they called it was a spout, where the water cascaded through the hedge, from a big spring further up. The neighbours brought their sheep here to be washed at the spout. They used to get a penny more for the washed wool.

The stream ran under the roadway to another field, where Mikie, when he was older, made a swimming pool, and all the neighbouring children used to go there in the summertime. They very quickly learnt to swim.

The house was old and two storied. The parish priest from Cushinstown lived there at the time of the 1798 rebellion, and there was a big granite stone just outside where he used to mount his horse.

There were three bedrooms upstairs, and downstairs were a parlour, a kitchen, dairy, and another bedroom. The kitchen had a large open fireplace; it was so big you could sit in the corners

ire, where there were forms for this purpose.
ı lovely on a cold winters night. There was a
e, which was driven by turning a handle on a
ich by means of a belt turned a smaller wheel,
beaters or fans around. You could soon have a
ith this, and all the cooking was done here. There
over the fire, on which hung skillets, frying pan and
a ba.   an. All the bread was made here. Gorse, of which there was abundance around the farm, was very good for getting a fire going. Timber was also used, and some coal.

Near the house were the kitchen garden and an orchard with some large apple trees. In the corner of it were huge laurels; they must have been there many years as they had branches the size of tree trunks. They were a constant attraction for the children, who played many games there, and enjoyed the swing, which was attached to the branches.

Mikie loved the springtime flowers; he had his own secret place, where the earliest violets grew around an old ash stump. He would bring the first ones in as a surprise for his mother. He loved the cowslips too, of which there were quite a few in the meadows. Below the orchard was a small bog. Mikie would dig out a few spits of this with a spade, and, when it had filled up with water, he rode bare back on the donkey and made it jump this small waterway. One day the donkey stumbled, and over it's head went Mikie.

Next to the bog was a hilly field, called Witty's. Mikie and his little sister Nancy had fun rolling from the top to the bottom of this.

They had a happy and carefree childhood.

The children had a walk of two miles to the school in Cushinstown. They loved to go in their bare feet in the summertime. On the way home they found birds nests, and picked wild strawberries and blackberries, when they were in season. They would be ready for their cooked meal when they reached home. This was usually colcannon, a meal made by mashing the potatoes and adding onion sliced very thinly, and then heated until the onions were soft. A plate of this with a big lump of home made butter in the middle was like ambrosia to the hungry children. They had plenty of milk to wash it down with.

One of the favourite games of the schoolboys was "Hunt the Fox". One boy would be the fox, and have a start across the fields; the others were the hounds and would try to catch him. One day Mikie was the fox, he ran so far avoiding his captors that he was late getting back to school, and was slapped by Master Murphy. The master must have thought that exercise was good, because every day he sent the boys on one hundred yard races up the road in their bare feet.

Their schooldays were at the time of the Black and Tans, but the boys saw no danger, and used to play tricks on the soldiers. One day they heard that the IRA had removed a mine which had been laid in the middle of the road, so they found an old tin and placed it in the hole, with a bit sticking out.

They were just coming out of school when an armoured car passed. The soldiers saw what they thought was a mine and opened fire, this caused great amusement to the little rascals. Another time, when the Tans were coming, the boys made holes in the bottom of tins, and placed a small amount of carbide inside. They then spat on it and tied down the tops with string. The carbide was lit through the holes in the bottom. The tops were then blown off the tins, making a noise like gunfire, and the soldiers started shooting at them as they ran along behind the hedge.

They thought it was great fun, which was until the day the dog was shot. Mikie and his friend Pat were walking along the Wexford road with Pats little dog, when the Tans came along and shot the poor little dog for no reason at all. They didn't feel like playing war games after that.

One day they had a nasty fright at home. The Ballymacar Bridge, which was quite near the farm, was blown up by the IRA, who then set up an ambush for the Black and Tans. When the soldiers came along there was such firing from the hill at one side of the farm, to the hill at the other side.

The soldiers thought the IRA were hiding in the farmhouse, and came storming up to the door. Mikie's mother was at home that day with only the children. They all came out in fear and trembling, but the soldiers left when they could find no enemies.

There was a stream flowing around part of the farm. The men cleaned this out in the summertime, the water being diverted onto the land for this purpose. Mikie used to catch the trout and eels, which were left stranded on the bed of the stream. He caught them with his hands and took them home to be fried. They had fish on the menu for a week.

A great day for them was the day the fat pig was killed. The spinsters sat around the fireplace making black pudding, white pudding, and sausages, while the men would be salting and cutting up the bacon, and putting it in a barrel. This would keep them going in meat for a long time. There would be another fat pig coming along when this was finished.

Mikie was about twelve years old when he left Cushintown to attend the Christian Brothers School in New Ross. The brothers were very good teachers. As they were building a new school at that time the boys went to the old poorhouse.

There was plenty of space there for football and hurling. They used to take a couple of cuts of bread for their dinners.

Mikies schooling was often interrupted by work at home. He only did one complete term, when he became top of the class. He was often away for up to five weeks at a time, hoeing mangolds, picking spuds, or some other seasonal job.

He was eventually forced to leave school at fourteen, when the man who drove the horses at the farm had to be let off as the wages became too high. Mikie and his two brothers received no wages. They only got the price of a packet of cigarettes and enough for the cinema on Sunday nights.

CHAPTER EIGHT
1926- 1947

Ballymacar Bridge, as it is now

Ballymacar was a mixed farm; corn and root crops were grown, milking cows were kept, as were sheep and pigs, and two brood mares. They also had, an Agriculture Department boar.
As well as Ballymacar they had an out - farm at Ballyrue, which was about five miles away. This was one of the farms they had in the Irishtown days.
In those days, after Mikie left school they had only a mowing machine for cutting the corn. The sheaves had to be bound by hand, before being put into stooks. It was later drawn into the haggard by horse and cart. In the fall, about the end of September, the thrashing machine came. That was a big day at the farm.
The thrashing machine arrived the night before. The two men in charge stayed the night, to be up early next morning. They would start getting up steam at five thirty, and at seven thirty they went into the kitchen for breakfast. At eight o'clock they were ready to blow the whistle for work to commence. Twenty five to thirty neighbours came to help. All these had to be fed, and so a couple of hams were cooked, a large skillet of potatoes, cabbage and bacon was produced.
The donkey was hitched into the cart with a water barrel on it. Mikie, in his younger days, had the job of hauling the water from the spout for the engine. He also had to rake the chaff.

There was a queer character, named Jack Burke, who used to go around with the thrasher. Mikie asked him how old was the thrashing machine, and he answered "twenty years". He then asked him how long he'd been going around with it. "Forty years" was the reply.

"You look young for your age" said Mikie, "you have hardly a grey hair". Jack replied "I put boot polish on my hair, and I put machine oil on my boots".

This Jack was intrigued with the old English sheepdog on the farm, and he would say "That's a great plan of a dog you've got there!"

The thrashing always ended up with a dance in the kitchen of the house. Local melodeon or fiddle players would supply the music, and a bucket of beer was always supplied, sometimes two! Songs were sung and tales told.

As the thrasher made its way around the neighbourhood all the men went with it to help. Sometimes it took a couple of months to finish the thrashing. They must have been very tired, as it is extremely hard work, and all the merriment at nights, but they all enjoyed the thrashing.

There were two areas of the farm called cnocs. They were areas that were covered with gorse. One was called the side cnoc, the other was about half an acre at the top of the hill.

The local hunts used to come and try to get the fox out of the gorse. There was great excitement when the hunt came.

The Master was a kind Englishman named Captain Farkin. He was connected with Johnstown Castle, and was a very popular person, well liked by the local people. You would have to be Irish to realise the significance of this, as the English landlords had treated them so badly in the past.

The countryside around Ballymacar was ideal for viewing the hounds. From the top of the hill you could see for ten miles around, and there were not too many large trees. In the distance Mount Leinster and Mount Brandon could be seen. While, nearby was Slieve Coillte, at the foot of which was the homeland of JF Kennedy's Great Grandfather, who left Ireland in the 1840s. Now there is a memorial park and large arboretum planted in President Kennedy's memory.

At the back of Ballymacar Hill, though not on the Rice land, was a fairy rath. This was a circular ditch enclosing about a quarter of an acre, in the middle of which were blackthorn bushes. Some people said they saw fairies there and heard fairy music. The children loved this place when they were small.

Mikie worked very hard on the farm, with his two brothers, Jack and James. James mainly worked with the horses, and broke in the young ones. These were Irish draft horses, a very strong breed, which were also used as hunters. Many of them were bought for police work in England, and also for the Queens horses. Mikie often went with James and the horses to work at Ballyrue. They also brought corn to the mill to be ground into flour. Their own flour was used for baking the bread.

Mikies oldest sister Maggie was married at this time, and most of the other girls were working in New Ross. Biddy was at home helping their mother. She often brought tea out to the fields where the men were working, no doubt some of her apple tarts too.

When the days work was done the boys usually made for the bridge, where most of the local lads gathered, and they often played skittles there. They sometimes made their way to local houses, where there would be dancing and singing in the kitchen. Hurling and football were also played, and Mikie did a lot of running.

On Sunday nights in the summertime there was often dancing at the crossroads in Ryleen or the Milebush. A stage was set up by the roadside, and a crowd would gather there. A melodeon usually provided the music, and they would dance until they were all tired out.

On other Sunday nights they would go to the pictures in New Ross. There was usually a queue to go in, and while waiting, the lads thought that it was great fun to push and get the whole queue moving backwards and forwards. When they got in they sat on hard forms in the pits, as these were the cheapest seats.

After a few years Jack left them to go to Chicago, where he stayed for about five years. Mikies father died in 1945, when he was well over ninety. He was still able to read, and he loved to be able to go and play cards in the little house by the bridge with his neighbours, right up until that time.

His mother died the following year, and as Jack had then returned from America and taken over the farm, Mikie crossed the Irish Sea, and that was how the two paths met.

PART TWO

Donegal Days

1973 – 1987

David with Charlie

CHAPTER NINE
1951 – 1977

Ballinamore

I am going to skip the next twenty, or so, years. They were very happy years. We had our three children, and our lives were very involved with bringing them up. We went nearly every year to Ireland for our holidays; we loved it more and more.
It was not until 1973 that we discovered Donegal. Mike was due to retire in 1977, so we were on the lookout for somewhere to live, as he always longed to return to Ireland.
We were touring around the west of Ireland, passing Mayo and Sligo, and hoped to reach Donegal by nightfall. As we passed through Sligo, with Ben Bulben on our right, away across the sea to our left were the mountains of Donegal, reaching down to Glencolumbkille. It is the most incredible first sight of Donegal.
We drove through Donegal town, as far as Glenties, where we stopped for petrol. We were told there of a nice place for bed and breakfast at Mellys Bar, about twelve miles along the road at a place called Meenagoland. We little thought, as we passed the little whitewashed houses of Fintown and Ballinamore that we should spend so many years there.
We reached our destination; it must have been a Sunday night, as there was a band playing in the lounge and a big crowd of people singing lovely Irish songs. Everyone made us welcome, as we squashed in with the rest.

At breakfast, the next morning, we were talking to Patrick, the landlord, of retiring to Ireland. He told us of a bit of land he had for sale up the road at Ballinamore. It sounded very cheap to us, and we could not believe it when he told us there were seventy nine acres.
As we were leaving to return home to England right away after breakfast, he said he would come along the road and show us. So we stopped at the gate at Ballinamore and saw our future home for the first time. We only went in a few hundred yards, and afterwards we discovered it was over a mile long. There was a roadway going up to the ruins of an old house. On one side of the roadway was the burn, in some places rippling along, and in others, falling in sparkling waterfalls over the mossy stones. We fell in love with it then and there, and bought it without seeing anymore. It was with great excitement the following year we went to examine our entire property. We felt like Christopher Columbus discovering some new lands. No one had lived on the farm for about thirty years, and it was in a dilapidated state. We did not mind, - we would start from scratch.
The land stretched in a long band from the River Finn at the bottom, to the top of Teivdeevan Hill. We made our way to the river, where we found a lovely deep pool with plenty of trout. There were reeds growing there, which made cover for curlews and herons, and in the winter, swans, which always come to the lake. Loch Shivnagh, the lake, turned into a river when it reached our boundary. There were plenty of Corncrakes too, although they disappeared, even here, in the space of a few years. We were amazed too, at all the wild flowers, which we used to see in England, but were growing more rare as each year passed. There were masses of wild orchids on the low lying ground, and a long stretch of meadow from the river up to the main road.
Across the road we followed the burn up to the ruins of the old house and the byres. The roofs were all fallen in, but we could see that wood was still quite firm. This wood had, in times past, been dug out of the bog, where it had been buried for many hundreds, or maybe thousands, of years. We followed the burn

up the hill. It was over a mile to the top, the burn having branched off about half way up. The top part of our land was unfenced and our boundary ran up to, what our neighbour informed us, were the "turtagi bainne". This was a most peculiar place, not unlike a lunar landscape. The very top of the hill was like a huge saucer filled with large turf banks and deep holes, which you could negotiate by jumping from place to place. When you were in the centre you could see nothing of the outside world, only this lunar landscape all around you.

When you were out of the turtagi there were about forty mountaintops completely surrounding you. We could see Mount Errigal, Donegal's highest mountain, Slieve Snaght, Aghla, the Bluestacks, and, of course, Scraigs, the one nearest Ballinamore, and many more. It was a magnificent sight, added to which, many lakes could be seen.

We were very pleased with our discoveries, and decided to get a house built as soon as possible, and also to get some fencing done, as animals were coming in from all sides.

This was all achieved by the time we came to live here, when we threw in our lot with the mountain farmers of Donegal.

CHAPTER TEN
1977 –1987

Going to Donegal was like going back thirty years to where I left off so many years before.
Our first friend, apart from Patrick and Nora at the pub, was Hughie. It was very difficult to understand what he said, even the locals could not understand him sometimes. He lived in a lovely old house across the hills, which had an open turf fireplace with the pots hanging from hooks above it.
Unfortunately, poor Hughie was the only member of his family left at home, with only his dog for company. For the companionship he missed so much he would go to Patrick's (Mellys Bar) after his hard days work.
He was an expert at putting up fences. They were always put up in dead straight lines, not an inch out of place. He came to help us with some of ours, and it was very hard on Hughie when we fenced the drive, which had a lovely curve up to the house. He had never done fencing on a curve before.
We used to love listening to Hughie's' tales. When he was a small boy of eight or nine he had to go off to a hiring fair in Strabane, which was about thirty miles away. He worked on a farm for six months, and these were very hard times for the girls and boys hired, they often didn't have a change of clothes until they came home. They were given six pounds for their six

months hard labour. Of course, they had to walk everywhere in those days. We heard how, at one time his mother did not have a clock, but she knew when it was time for the children to leave for school by the shadow of the sun on a stone outside their whitewashed home.

There were lots of card games at Patrick's, among which "Twenty fives" was always played. Hughie was an expert, and no matter how many whiskies he had taken his playing was always good, and he was a perfect gentleman.

One of his last jobs was working for the council, making a hikers way across the mountains, from a few miles outside of Ballybofey to Mount Eske, near Donegal Town. They had to put posts every so many yards to mark the way. It meant carrying heavy posts miles across the mountains. There was a waterfall near the route called The Grey Mares Tail. Hughie wanted to show us this, as well as his handiwork. So one day we set off. It was a beautiful day as we clambered up the mountainside, with lovely views of Mount Eske as we went. We were amazed to see the Grey Mares Tail. The water seemed to come down a long way, like a white mist, or a huge white lace curtain.

Not long after this poor Hughie became ill. He had such a hard life from all the soaking in the cold rain, and having no warm fire or cooked dinner waiting for him at night. After a short while we were sad to lose our friend.

At the funeral in Fintown church, during the service a swallow came in and flew around the coffin like some wild spirit. It was very fitting for poor Hughie. It was the only time I ever saw one there.

We had many friends. Amongst them was John, our next door neighbour. He was intensely fond of Ballinamore, and would never hear a word said against it. He had a heart of gold, and was always ready to give a helping hand. He lived alone with his two collie dogs, Dolly and Colliebeag. Through John we soon made friends with his sister Nora and her husband Con, who lived over the hills near Hughie. They too, lived in an old house. The only sign of modernization was the iron kitchen range.

To reach their house you had to leave the road and travel down a very steep lane, to find the house nestling beneath the trees. It was the happiest house I was ever in, there was always a welcome. Con loved his house and would not have anything changed. It was in the style of all the old farmhouses of Donegal. You entered the door, which was a half door, the bottom half could remain shut to keep out the hens and sheep etc. which were outside in the "street", as it was called (bearing in mind the remote location).

Inside was a large room, which was the kitchen, where there was always a warm turf fire, with big pots of hot water and spuds on top. There was the dresser with all the bright delph, and the table and homemade, painted chairs. By the side of the fire was a curtained bed, at the back of a long wooden seat. The rakers (as the neighbourly callers are referred to in Donegal), usually sat on this seat. The men nearly always sat that side; the ladies sat near the table the other side. There was always a St. Bridget's Cross on the wall, as in most Donegal houses. They were hung in every room and in the byres. Con was an expert at making them, he would use green and white rushes sometimes to make a pattern. On St. Bridget's Eve nearly every family made the crosses.

On one wall was the ring board, and most nights there was great competing at this. If there was a lot of rakers there would be teams made up, and it was great sport. The house also contained a small room that was a dairy and larder, and a large room the other side of the door, which was usually referred to as the "room". It had a lovely open fireplace with old tiles around and a mirror above. There were double beds, tail to tail at one side, completely curtained off. All the old houses I saw were of the same pattern. They were nearly always repainted inside yearly, usually in bright colours. The outside was whitewashed annually; especial attention was given to the chimneys.

Nora always made her own bread. She would buy a sack of flour, which would last a couple of weeks. She never let anyone away without a slice of this delicious bread and a cup of tea.

Ownie was another of our friends. I do not know how to describe poor Ownie. He lived next door to John, and was like a modern day Peter Pan. No one could ever remember his being any different. He would never miss a party, a dance or a wake. He was away every Saturday night to the disco, twelve miles away in Glenties, with what must have been, the third generation of youngsters.

He could never be serious; he loved a bit of fun more than anything else, but was also kindness itself, and would do anything for his friends. He loved flowers, and would usually arrive with a bunch, or maybe a bulb or a few seeds.

Nearby lived Paddy and Nellie and their three lovely lassies. They used to invite us for Christmas tea if we were on our own. The girls would entertain us with lovely Irish music. They always played "The Coolin", which was everyone's favourite. These were a few of our friends, but there were many more.

The area we lived in was an Irish speaking one, but everyone would speak in English to us. In Fintown church the mass was always said in Irish. There was an Irish college in Ballinamore, where students went in the summertime from all parts of Ireland to learn the Gaelic. They built on an extension to it a little while after we arrived, and the opening of it was celebrated with a dance. It was supposed to start at nine, so we duly arrived on time to find the band playing away with all their might, but there were no people, so after a while the band went off, I suppose to the pub. Then the people came but there was no band. Eventually the band came back. Drinks were served at a makeshift bar. They had no water there, so if anyone wanted water in their whiskey the lady in charge had to go off to the ladies for it, we thought that very funny. The night ended up in a fight, it was hilarious altogether. We saw very few fights the whole time we were in Donegal.

The main topics of conversation around our part of the world, in their seasons, were lambs, turf, harvesting (as haymaking was called), and the prices in the local marts.

Everyone cut their own turf, enough for the whole years supply. The first years we were there we used to cut the turf about halfway up our hill. The turf there was four or five feet deep, and it was hard and black like coal when it was dry. We would spend a few days digging. John always helped us, and we helped him in return, and some of our other neighbours helped sometimes.

We had to wait until all our fear of frost had gone, as if it got frosted before it was dry it would all crumble up and be useless. It was much easier if there was one person digging, one throwing it up on the bank, and another person with a turf barrow wheeling it out onto the open ground to dry in the wind and sun. There was not room at the top of the bank, with so many spits depths of turf to spread it singly. After this was accomplished everyone would be praying for fine weather to dry the turf. When it was dry one side it had to be turned over. When it was sufficiently dry then it was all footed. About four turves were stood on end, with one on the top, until it was fairly dry. Then it was put into large stacks to weather until carted home. Sometimes, if the weather was bad it would take the whole summer to get it dry, and then the fine weather would coincide with the haymaking. It was really lovely up the hill working at the turf in fine weather, the larks were singing overhead, and you could see the neighbours busy too. If you wanted to sit and take a rest there were the most marvellous views of lakes and mountains all around. At the bottom of the turf banks were tree stumps which had been growing there hundreds of years ago, before the turf was formed, we even found fir cones in the bog.
Alas, even Donegal is changing to modern ways, and machines are digging most of the turf now.
We had no byres when we first went there, so could not get many animals straight away. Apart from our two collie dogs and two cats, which we brought with us, the only animal we had for a while was a wee lamb. It was a motherless lamb John had in his kitchen, and he gave her to me. I called her Ba Ba. She was our lucky mascot, and was like a mother to all the other sheep we ever had. We bought another lamb later to keep her company, which also became a pet, and we called her Timmy.
One evening a man came around selling calves. We said we would buy them, but had no food for them. We needed powdered milk, calf nuts and hay. We were told this would be no problem if we went to the post office a few miles down the road. So away we went at ten o clock at night to the post office and bought all the food we needed. We had rebuilt the old byre by then, so we soon got a small herd of cows and were farmers again.

We were lucky with everything we did. In, fact, Hughie said we were as lucky as two black cats! We found white heather growing up the hill, so maybe that was it.

After a number of years we found the haymaking was getting too much for us, and decided to just keep sheep. I was mostly in charge of them. Ba Ba and Timmy had had quite a few lambs by then, so we had quite a little flock. We bought a few more and we were sheep farmers.

Most of the sheep around our part of the world were black-faced mountain sheep. They were as wild as their mountains, not to be compared with the docile sheep of the lowlands. Every time they had to go into the house for dosing, or clipping, or any of the other things you have to do for sheep, it was like a rodeo, they would never go in but for the dogs!

As we usually helped John with his sheep (he often had over a hundred) as well as our own, we were kept pretty busy. The worst period was getting the lambs in for the first time. They would be from newly born up to about two months old. John would drive all his sheep down from the hill; it was just like driving rabbits! They were so wild, that if one escaped, they would all be gone, and away back up the hill again.

When we finally got them into the yard the ewes were dosed and the lambs marked. John's had a red mark and ours had a blue mark on the shoulder. We got to know all the marks around the area. Before John got his sheep-dipping tank built we used to drive the sheep a couple of miles over the hills to a council dip.

One day when we went there no one remembered to take a decent bucket, and the tank needed 200 gallons of water. Across the road and down a steep bank was a small well, so taking some buckets that we found there, that were full of holes, we made a mad scramble up the bank and across the road, only to find they were almost empty again! John then had the bright idea of using plastic bags, but they were full of holes too. In the end someone had to go home for buckets.

It was always a fiasco every time we did things with the sheep. My sheep, which were such pets most of the time, were worse than any to get in, because they would take no notice of the dogs. One day John wanted a hand to get his sheep and lambs across the road and into the fields below. The only way to get lambs across is to make sure they are with their mothers, as once parted the lambs cannot be driven and the sheep are too busy with the fresh grass to worry about their offspring. John's gate opened both ways, and by mistake, he opened it inwards. Ownie, (who had been commandeered to help) and I had instructions not to dare let the ewes along the road until all the lambs were out of the gate. The ewes rushed into the road, but about a dozen lambs got stuck behind the gate. Owney and I were nearly frantic trying to stop the ewes that wanted to get to the grass. A lot of traffic had come along by this time; we were too busy to worry about them. Most of the sheep got past us, in spite of our maniacal behaviour trying to stop them. John managed to get all the lambs out, bar one, and all the traffic was able to go on again. It was only afterwards I began wondering what the people in the cars must have thought of us. Then the race was on to find the missing lamb, which was making it's way back up the hill by that time. We managed to run it into a pile of brushwood in the end, and it was caught and put back in with the ewes. Peace was restored again.

We had an American girl student staying with us once on a cultural holiday scheme. These students were supposed to live as the families they were staying with, and one day the sheep needed dipping. Kathleen, as her name was, said she would like to help. She came out in a spotless white suit, but anyone who has dipped sheep knows what a smell there is to sheep dip, not to mention all the manure. John gave her the job of preventing the sheep that had already been dipped from jumping over the side, until the dip which was on their fleeces had run back into the tank, and also, to help with the counting.

Poor Kathleen had never been near a sheep before-she was a sorry spectacle. She surely learnt a lot about Donegal and its inhabitants that day!

Lambing time is the hardest, and sometimes heartbreaking. So many dangers lie in wait for the poor little lambs. Sometimes the crows would pick out their eyes, and even their tongues, before they were born.

They seemed to usually arrive at night, and if it was a very hard frost they would be frozen to death, especially if they were twins. One morning it took me two hours to find one of the ewes. There was a very heavy white frost and she had got on her back, and could not be seen against the frost. Her lamb was partly born, but its head was frozen solid. The ewe soon recovered after I pulled the lamb and put her the right way up again. Sometimes I would put a ewe in the house at night to have her lamb, this practice was very much frowned upon by our neighbours, but I saved many sheep and lambs that way.

Some of the sheep were much too wild to get anywhere near a house when they were lambing. There was a lady living in a towns land near us who was wonderful with sheep. All the farmers in our neighbourhood who had trouble with lambing would go to her for help. We had to fetch her on a couple of occasions. One time it was because a sheep couldn't lamb. She managed to turn the lamb around inside the sheep, but had great difficulty getting one leg out, to which she then tied a string. We had to pull the leg so hard, but in the end the lamb was born safely. No one could believe the lamb was still living, though the poor leg was stretched longer than the others, and appeared to be broken. After a few days it still could not use the leg, so over to Con we went with the lamb.

Con was marvellous with lambs that had broken legs. He would feel the leg so gently and find just the right place to put on the splint. He was so careful to get just the right piece of wood, and Nora would help him bandage it up. All this took place in the kitchen. The lamb was then put down on the floor, and it would take its shaky steps around the kitchen. I called this lamb Peggy, because of its peg leg. After a few weeks it was completely cured. Con mended several lambs legs for us. One lamb was quite big, when it caught its leg in some wire and broke it.

Con loved his animals very much. Once, he bought a few ewe lambs, and sold a couple of them to me, as he didn't want so many. We kept these lambs all the winter and were very pleased with them. One day, we went over to see Con, and there were his lambs, all killed by dogs. It was really heartbreaking to see their mangled bodies. Poor Con had to go with the wheelbarrow to pick up the remains; tears were not far from his eyes.

One day, John came running over to tell us that there was a dog worrying sheep on our hill. I ran all up that steep hill. There was poor Timmy trying to protect her twins, and could not keep the dog from both of them at once. She was beating at him with her front hoofs, and butting him with her horns. I only reached her in the nick of time, she fell down exhausted, once she knew her babies were safe.

I reared several of John's motherless lambs. One of these we called Charlie. He was a little darling, and was petted by everyone. He was quite big, and out on the hill with the other sheep, when the grandchildren came to stay. All the children made a great fuss of him, but for some reason he took a dislike to my grandson David. David was about seven years old then, and every time he went anywhere on the farm he was charged by Charlie. The only way David could advance at all was by holding on tight to Charlie's little horns, and never letting go!

We also had another unusual sheep from John, which we called Bambi (all our sheep had names). Bambi thought she was a dog, or something; definitely not a sheep. She never stayed near any other sheep all her life. If they were at the top of the hill, she would be down, and visa versa. One day David was walking along by the brae when suddenly, over his head, went a flying object. It was Bambi!

She was a real harum-scarum of a mother, the poor lambs had to look out for themselves, and if they got lost, she would never bleat to them. She had a special place where she used to sleep at night. It was a sort of hollowed out bank by the side of the burn, the most dangerous place on the farm for wee lambs. Many a time, I had to rescue them from the swirling waters, after we had a lot of rain. Sheep are all great characters; there are no two alike. People say they are silly animals. If they ever took the trouble to get to know their little ways, they would realise their mistake.

Uranium

We had not long been in Donegal when uranium was discovered in our area. A lot of people, not realising the danger, thought it would be a great thing, and would create plenty of employment. There were helicopters going around daily, taking readings, or what ever it is they do. The whole area around us was surveyed, and stakes stuck in everywhere.

There were a team of men going around, systematically testing the land. Three of these men stayed with us one time. They brought their samples home with them and sorted them out on the kitchen table. I was getting a bit alarmed at that, but we didn't know so much about it at that time. One night, they came home and told us we should use all our money to buy shares in their company, they seemed quite exited.

There were quite a lot of anti-uranium meetings held at this time, and some of their machinery was broken up. Whether it was that, or whether they all ran out of money, we never found out, but they all disappeared.

The people in the Donegal hills work very hard, and the weather is so extreme they have to be tough to survive. Maybe now, it's not so bad, with all the machinery to help them. They often have big welts on their hands in the wintry weather, and sore feet. Yet, come Sunday nights (and other nights too), away a lot of them go to the dance, or the sing song, sore hands and feet forgotten.

We were lucky in the place our house was situated; we were on a main road. We were near the mart; and from our window we could see the Millwheel, where there was a lovely floor for dancing. Some people had to travel miles for these things. Some would even come from the North for a nice night out.

We had a lovely band from our area. When Paddy played the fiddle, and Sean sang, you just could not keep from dancing. The first time we met Paddy was when we had just moved in. He was a friend of the plumber and the electrician, who usually put in their appearances about ten o'clock at night. One night Paddy came with the plumber and played his lovely music, while his friend was working, until well after midnight. We wondered

what our friends in England would have thought about this, where the plumbers usually finish at five o'clock sharp.
St. Patrick's Day is a great day in Donegal; everyone went to mass with a big bunch of shamrock pinned to their hats or coats. Some years the shamrock was very difficult to find. However, Ownie always found some of it somewhere to distribute to all his friends. There were big parties in Dungloe and other towns. In the evening there was music and dancing in all the bars and dancehalls. There was quite a lot of whiskey drunk that night. The dancing was wild, as usual, and often ended with people holding each other up. Great fun was had by all!
Every year the parish priest in Fintown, which was our nearest church, would say the stations in some of the houses. This was announced in church without any prior warning. It was held twice in our house, while we were there, and at most of our neighbours' houses. There was much preparation, sometimes the whole house was repapered or painted inside; much baking was done, and the altar was prepared with a spotless white cloth, flowers, candlesticks and silver bowls. This was how it went in a neighbours house: Everyone gathered about seven o'clock, when it was supposed to start. Most of the men stayed in the hall, while about twenty or so women crowded into the kitchen, waiting for the priest to arrive.
Everyone was speaking in whispers, except Mike and one of the men. Various surmises were made as to where the priest had got. Heated argument started between two of the women about where the priest was making the old peoples calls that night. At eight o'clock there was still no priest, and everyone was running out of whispered conversation, getting stiff from sitting on half a chair.
Eventually the priest arrived. He then heard confessions, which took a long time, as the priest, who was a lovely man, would have long conversations with everyone. The mass was said in Irish in the sitting room. There was not room for all, so some knelt in the passage, and the priest brought the communion out there. Afterwards we were invited to tea. A big spread was put on with lovely cakes and home made bread. The priest enjoyed

the homemade bread the best; maybe he had no one to make him any at home. There were about forty people there

The loveliest mass I was ever at was in John's kitchen. His nephew was a priest in Scotland, and when he came to John for his holidays he sometimes said mass in Fintown. One Sunday he was not needed there so he said it at home. John's collie dogs always lay under the kitchen table, which, was made into an altar. A few neighbours came along too. It was so simple, and so lovely, kneeling on the flagstone floor in front of the fire, so near to the priest, and with Dolly and Jessie so good under the table (Colliebeag was no longer there). No cathedral could compare with it.

Wakes were still very much kept up in Donegal. I had never been to one before, and was never very happy about going to them, but it was the custom, and when in Rome............. There were usually big crowds coming and going over the one or two nights the wakes were held. If there were a lot of people, you would just go in and say a prayer at the coffin, and after a short while go out to the kitchen for tea and sandwiches. If there were not a big crowd you usually sat a while with the dead person. I was amazed that people could just carry on an ordinary conversation, maybe about sheep, or chickens, in the company of the dead person, as though they were still able to take part. The priest always came to say the rosary at midnight. Some people always sat up all night. I think the wakes really help the bereaved people more than anything else, as they know they are not alone and that the whole neighbourhood cares about them. Some members of the family, or friends, usually dig the grave, and fill it in afterwards. The children, however small, take their part, helping at the wake and attending the funeral. There was no whispering or keeping the children in the dark about what is going on, as there is in England, and they learn to accept death as something natural. Babies' wakes are most sad, and sometimes their little brothers or sisters carry the coffin at the funeral. Children are called wains in that area, or, 'the wee ones'.

During the eleven years we lived in Donegal so many things changed, most people got television; new houses were built, and most of the old thatched houses disappeared, and many farmers got hay barns.

When we first went there, the haymaking, or harvest as it was called, was very hard work for all. Some people still mowed the 'paircs', as the fields were called, with scythes, but most got someone with a tractor to do the job. Then the hay was shaken out, almost immediately, by hand, and put into laps, which were tiny heaps of hay rolled around in the arms. I was never any good at making them, but some people could quickly do whole fields. The weather was never fine for very long in our hills, and the laps were a great help as they could easily be tipped over on a fine day. Then the hay was put into bigger heaps, called hand cocks, and from there it progressed into tram cocks, which were like miniature hayricks. They had to be tied down to keep them from blowing away. They stayed in the fields until all the haymaking was finished, and then brought in, lifted by a tractor onto a sweep at the back. They never broke up, and were sometimes carried miles along the road. These were all dumped like enormous mushrooms some place near the byres, and were made into even bigger ricks called peaks. After this was done, rushes had to be cut in sufficient quantities to thatch them, and this had to be all securely tied with ropes to keep them safe in the gales.

So the work involved in haymaking in Donegal, all down the years, was really a mammoth job, with, maybe, only half an hour's sunshine in a day, or even a week. They don't know themselves now, with tractors and hay barns.

Con was a really good farmer, and always got everything in readiness before doing any job.

To his amazement one morning, on being awakened by an unusual noise, he saw one of his tramcocks passing the window. The tractor driver had been given the wrong name. Someone had wanted him real early before going to work, but they were kept waiting while all of Con's hay was brought in. We all had a good laugh afterwards.

Many were the happy hours we spent with Con and Nora. The 'crack' was always good there. Sometimes the kitchen was full of 'rakers', tales were told of the old times, and sometimes songs were sung.
Every Sunday night we were away to the dances, and when we came back Nora would make the tea.
Alas, our happy times came to an end with dear Con's sudden death. Poor Nora was heartbroken; they had been together so many years.
So many of our friends were now gone, and progress began taking over. There was a big road scheme for our road, and the council came and cut down all the trees below the house. They altered the course of the burn, so it washed away the banks by our drive, all for their road widening.

The years were taking their toll on us too, so reluctantly, we left dear Donegal, to move another two hundred and fifty miles away to Wexford, which was Mikies birthplace.
We will never see the like again to all those friendly people in the hills of Donegal.

EPILOGUE
1989

The farms of home lie lost in Even,
I see far off the steeple stand
West and away from here to Heaven
Still is the land

There if I go no girl will greet me
No friend will hollo from the hill
No dog run down the yard to greet me
The land is still

The land is still by farm and steeple
And still for me the land will stay
There I was friends with perished people
And there lie they

AE Housemsan

I made a return visit to the old home and all the old familiar places. I did not like anything I saw very much.
As the train passed through Wales and England, I could not believe the numbers of sheep that I saw. There were enormous flocks everywhere. Even at Budden's Lane there were flocks of sheep, an unheard of thing in the old days, when they were only kept on the higher, drier land.
What will happen to those bleating millions if the bottom drops out of the market?
Another curious thing I noticed were all the rooks, they seemed to have increased like the sheep. Even around Buddens, there were rooks nests in many of the trees, the nearest ones used to be in Melbury churchyard, where the young rooks were shot at every year, and made into rook pies. The old people said they would not come back if they were not shot. I wonder if modern farming methods are more congenial to rooks.

It made me very sad to see the cows around Melbury. They are just numbers now, with large plastic labels in their ears, and their horns all taken off. The Holstein breed seems to have taken over from the shorthorns and Devon's of the old days. They all have worried looking faces, that old contented look no longer there. Gone are all the dear character cows of the old days. The farms support three times the number they used to.

It seems pollution and threats to the environment are everywhere. There is all this talk of over-production; if only the farmers could understand there is no need for so much work and worry. They have three times as many calvings to contend with, and all the extra vets bills; Three times as much milking, washing up and manure hauling. There are slurry tanks polluting the earth, vast bills for fertilizers, weed killers and foodstuffs.

In the old days we had only a third of the work with the cows. We were entirely self-supporting in the summertime, with only small cake bills in the winter. What profit we made did not go to pay those enormous bills. We also, to my knowledge, never had any deficiency diseases among the cattle. They had all the meadow grass, containing sweet herbs, to feed on. The grass was not blown up by constant dressings of artificial fertilizers.

There are a few people that are environment conscious, but they are very much the minority.

However, there are still some lovely things. I still heard the cuckoo calling, and although most of the primroses have gone, the lane is still a picture, with bluebells, campions, cowparsley and mayflowers. There are still many rabbits, and badgers and foxes are on the prowl at night as in the days of yore.

My last points of call were the two churchyards, Melbury and Compton. They are in the most delightful of spots, with the rolling hills around them.

I said hello, goodbye to all my friends, there are so many of them. The happy, smiling faces I remembered from so long ago.

Edna Rice
New Ross
Co. Wexford
1989

Irish Draft Foal

James, Mikie and Jack

Stepping the Light Fantastic

Fun at the Thrashing

Corn at Ballymacar

John Rice's Irishtown house

Cross where John Rice was shot

The house, now deserted at Ballymacar

The Irishtown pub where Mike's mother lived

Mountain top, Ballinamore

Turf digging, old style

John and Mike in the hayfield

Turf digging, new style

Bringing in the hay

Ownie

Building the Peaks

Hay time in Ballinamore

Bambi

David, with Charlie